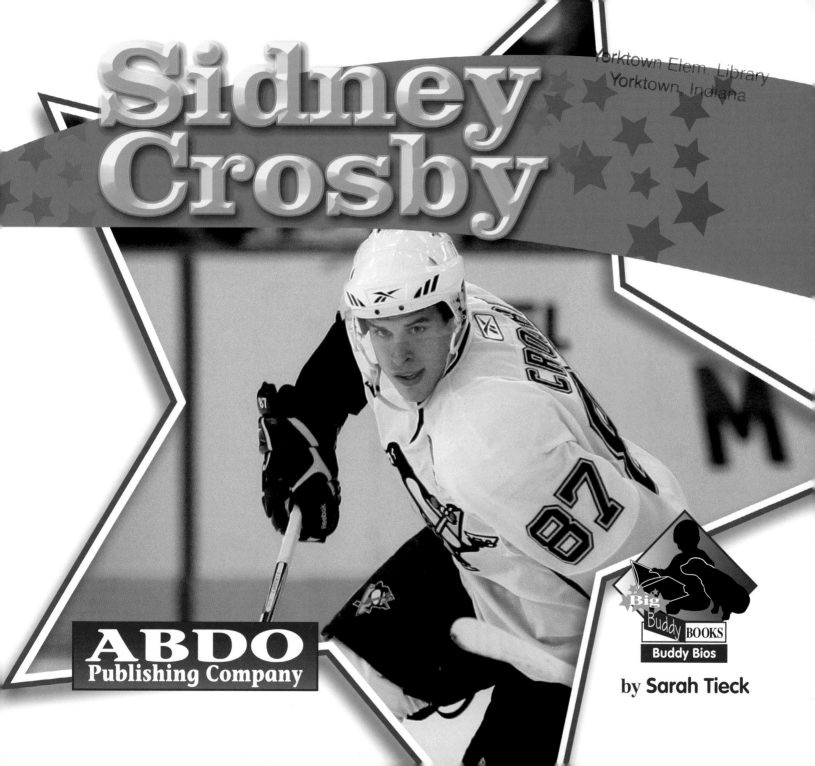

Sidney Crosby

ABDO
Publishing Company

Big Buddy BOOKS
Buddy Bios

by Sarah Tieck

VISIT US AT
www.abdopublishing.com

Published by ABDO Publishing Company, 8000 West 78th Street, Edina, Minnesota 55439.

Printed in the United States of America, North Mankato, Minnesota.
102010
012011
PRINTED ON RECYCLED PAPER

Coordinating Series Editor: Rochelle Baltzer
Contributing Editors: Megan M. Gunderson, BreAnn Rumsch, Marcia Zappa
Graphic Design: Maria Hosley
Cover Photograph: *AP Photo*: Frank Franklin II.
Interior Photographs/Illustrations: *AP Photo*: AP Photo (p. 23), Paul Chiasson, CP (p. 23), Mike Dembeck/The Canadian Press (p. 7), David Duprey (p. 12), Andre Forget, Halifax Dailey News via The Canadian Press (p. 5), Frank Gunn, CP (p. 17), Jonathan Hayward (pp. 15, 25, 26), Chris O'Meara (p. 24), Gene J. Puskar (p. 29), Paul Sancya (p. 19), Matt Slocum (p. 20), Adrian Wyld, CP (p. 23); *Getty Images*: Bruce Bennett (p. 9), Jiri Kolis (p. 12), Dave Sanford/Getty Images for NHL (p. 11).

Library of Congress Cataloging-in-Publication Data

Tieck, Sarah, 1976-
  Sidney Crosby : hockey champion / Sarah Tieck.
    p. cm. -- (Big buddy biographies)
  ISBN 978-1-61714-702-9
  1. Crosby, Sidney, 1987---Juvenile literature. 2. Hockey players--Canada--Biography--Juvenile literature. I. Title.
  GV848.5.C76T54 2011
  796.962092--dc22
  [B]
                          2010037637

Sidney
Crosby

Contents

Hockey Star

Sidney Crosby is famous for his sports skills. He plays hockey in the National Hockey League (NHL). Sidney plays for the Pittsburgh Penguins. He also played for Team Canada during the 2010 Olympics. Sidney is very talented!

Sidney plays center for the Penguins.

5

CANADA

Quebec

GULF OF SAINT LAWRENCE

New Brunswick

Maine

Cole Harbour

USA

Nova Scotia

ATLANTIC OCEAN

Family Ties

Sidney Patrick Crosby was born in Cole Harbour, Nova Scotia, Canada, on August 7, 1987. His parents are Trina and Troy Crosby. Sidney has a younger sister named Taylor.

Trina, Taylor, and Troy (*left to right*) have supported Sidney's hockey dreams.

Growing Up

While Sidney was growing up, the Crosbys enjoyed sports. When Sidney was three, he learned how to ice-skate.

Sidney soon found he loved hockey. He practiced often. His dad encouraged him to do his best.

By age five, Sidney was playing in youth hockey leagues. He was a strong player. So, young Sidney moved up to teams with older kids.

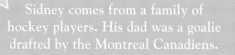

Sidney comes from a family of hockey players. His dad was a goalie drafted by the Montreal Canadiens.

Soon, Sidney began traveling to training camps. There, **professional** players recognized his skills. Some even stayed in touch with him.

In 2002, Sidney left home to play hockey at Shattuck-St. Mary's School in Faribault, Minnesota. There, he became a stronger player. In 2003, his team won a U.S. National **Championship**!

Sidney is close friends with NHL player Jack Johnson (*right*). Jack went to Shattuck-St. Mary's School with Sidney.

Sidney scored a goal at the 2004 World Junior Championships. He was the youngest Canadian player ever to do this!

Young Star

In 2003, Sidney was **drafted** by a team in the Quebec Major Junior Hockey League. That year, Sidney was named **Rookie** of the Year and Most **Valuable** Player. And, he won Major Junior Player of the Year for the Canadian Hockey League!

Sidney played for Team Canada in the 2004 World Junior **Championships**. He was one of five 16-year-olds ever to play for Canada.

Going Pro

The 2004–2005 season was another strong year for Sidney. He was named Major Junior Player of the Year for a second time.

Many **professional** hockey teams wanted Sidney to play for them. So, he entered the 2005 NHL **draft**. Sidney was the first player picked! The Pittsburgh Penguins chose him for their team.

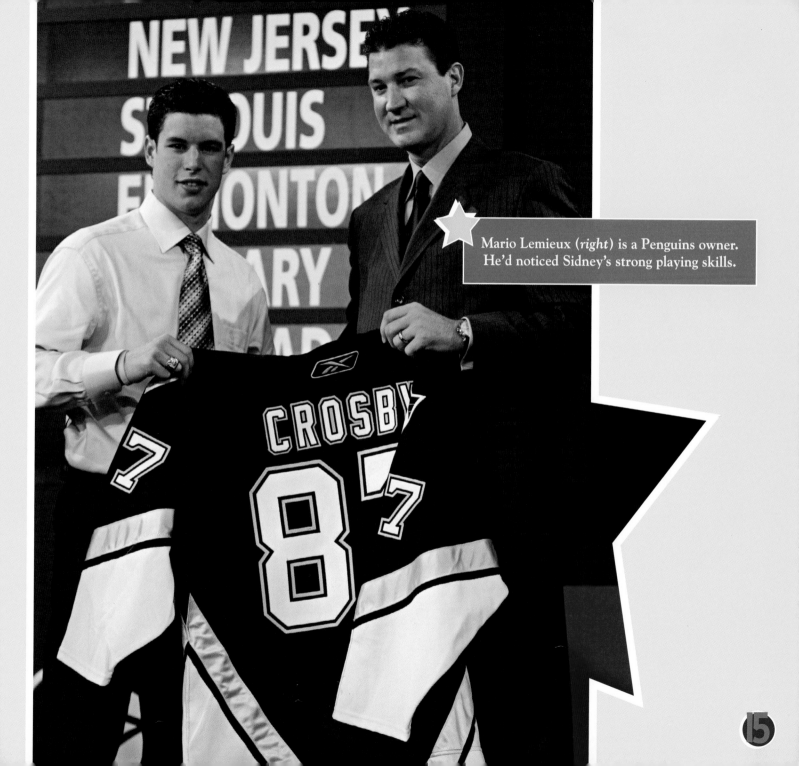

Mario Lemieux (*right*) is a Penguins owner. He'd noticed Sidney's strong playing skills.

Famous Athlete

During Sidney's rookie season, the Penguins struggled. But, Sidney played well. He became the youngest person to score more than 100 points in a season!

The 2006–2007 season was a stronger one. The Penguins went to the play-offs for the Stanley Cup! They didn't win, but the team played their best. That season, Sidney received three important awards for his skills.

In 2007, Sidney won the trophy for the most valuable player (*left*). Other players chose him for a top hockey player award (*center*). And, he earned a trophy for being the league's top scorer (*right*).

After the 2006–2007 season, Sidney became a team captain. During the 2007–2008 season, Sidney got hurt. Still, the Penguins made it to the **play-offs**.

In the play-offs, Sidney helped the team advance to the Stanley Cup finals! But, they lost to the Detroit Red Wings.

In the 2008–2009 season, the Penguins made it to the Stanley Cup finals again. So did the Red Wings. This time, the Penguins won! It was an important victory for Sidney and his team.

At 21, Sidney was the youngest
NHL captain to win the Stanley Cup.

As a member of Team Canada, Sidney wore a red and white jersey with a maple leaf on it.

Team Canada

Sidney wanted to play hockey in the Olympic Games. In 2010, the Winter Olympics were held in Vancouver, British Columbia, Canada. Sidney was very excited when he was chosen to play for Team Canada!

The Olympic Games

The Olympic Games are a famous sports **competition**. People from around the world compete to win Olympic events.

First-place winners receive gold **medals**. Silver medals are given to second-place winners. And, third-place winners receive bronze medals.

Ice hockey has been an Olympic sport since the 1920s. One of the most famous Olympic hockey teams was the 1980 U.S. men's team. They beat the Soviet Union in a game that became known as the "Miracle on Ice."

There were 15 types of events in the 2010 Winter Olympics. These included figure skating (*above*) and speed skating (*right*).

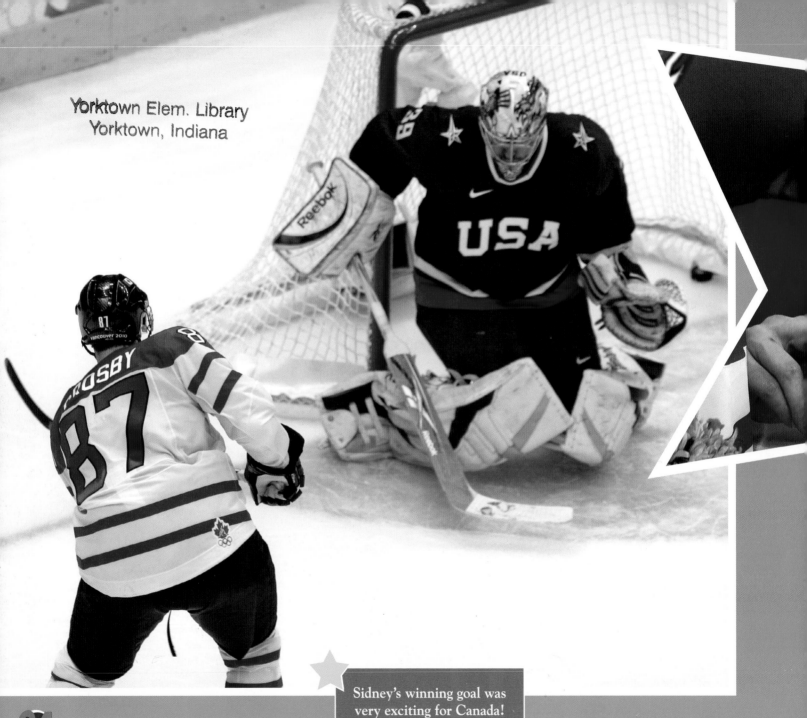

Sidney's winning goal was very exciting for Canada!

Sidney felt very proud to earn a gold medal. He also received $20,000 for winning. Sidney donated the money to charity to help others in Nova Scotia.

Winning Goal

Team Canada did well in Vancouver. They played against Team USA for the gold **medal**.

When time ran out, the score was tied at 2–2. So, the game went into overtime. Sidney scored the winning goal! Team Canada won 3–2.

Sidney is very well known. Fans often take his picture and ask for his autograph.

A Pro's Life

Sidney stays busy working to improve his skills. He practices with his team. And, he works out often to stay in top condition.

Sidney also attends public events and meets fans. Reporters **interview** him for magazines and television.

Sidney has a house in Cole Harbour. He spends his free time there. He likes to hang out with his friends and family.

Buzz

After the Olympics, Sidney returned to the United States. In 2010, the Penguins went to the **play-offs** for the fourth year in a row! They played their best, but they lost to the Montreal Canadiens.

Sidney and his team continue to work hard. Fans are excited to see what's next for rising star Sidney Crosby!

Steel

Snapshot

★**Name**: Sidney Patrick Crosby

★**Birthday**: August 7, 1987

★**Birthplace**: Cole Harbour, Nova Scotia, Canada

★**Turned professional**: 2005

★**Plays for**: Pittsburgh Penguins

★**Position**: Center

★**Number**: 87

Important Words

championship a game, a match, or a race held to find a first-place winner.

competition (kahm-puh-TIH-shuhn) a contest between two or more persons or groups. To compete is to take part in a competition.

draft an event during which sports teams choose new players. To be drafted is to be chosen by a sports team as a player.

interview to ask someone a series of questions.

medal an award for success.

play-off a set of games leading to a final match to find a winner.

professional (pruh-FEHSH-nuhl) working for money rather than for pleasure.

rookie a first-year player in a professional sport.

valuable of great use or service.

Web Sites

To learn more about Sidney Crosby, visit ABDO Publishing Company online. Web sites about Sidney Crosby are featured on our Book Links page. These links are routinely monitored and updated to provide the most current information available.

www.abdopublishing.com

Index

L: 4.1

p: 0.5